AMAZING STRUCTURES
SKYSCRAPERS

by Rebecca Pettiford

po**g**o

Ideas for Parents and Teachers

Pogo Books let children practice reading informational text while introducing them to nonfiction features such as headings, labels, sidebars, maps, and diagrams, as well as a table of contents, glossary, and index.

Carefully leveled text with a strong photo match offers early fluent readers the support they need to succeed.

Before Reading

- "Walk" through the book and point out the various nonfiction features. Ask the student what purpose each feature serves.
- Look at the glossary together. Read and discuss the words.

Read the Book

- Have the child read the book independently.
- Invite him or her to list questions that arise from reading.

After Reading

- Discuss the child's questions. Talk about how he or she might find answers to those questions.
- Prompt the child to think more. Ask: What is the biggest skyscraper you have ever seen?

Pogo Books are published by Jump!
5357 Penn Avenue South
Minneapolis, MN 55419
www.jumplibrary.com

Library of Congress Cataloging-in-Publication Data

Pettiford, Rebecca, author.
 Skyscrapers / by Rebecca Pettiford.
   pages cm. – (Amazing structures)
 Audience: Ages 7-9.
 Includes bibliographical references and index.
 ISBN 978-1-62031-210-0 (hardcover: alk. paper) –
 ISBN 978-1-62496-297-4 (ebook)
 1. Skyscrapers–Juvenile literature. I. Title.
 NA6230.P48 2015
 720.483–dc23

                                    2014042535

Series Editor: Jenny Fretland VanVoorst
Series Designer: Anna Peterson
Photo Researcher: Anna Peterson

Photo Credits: All photos by Shutterstock except:
Alamy, 11; Getty, 18-19, 23; iStock, cover; joyfull/
Shutterstock.com; junrong/Shutterstock.com;
Rahhal/Shutterstock.com; stockelements/
Shutterstock.com; SuperStock, 16-17;
Thinkstock, 6-7, 1.

Printed in the United States of America at Corporate Graphics in North Mankato, Minnesota.

TABLE OF CONTENTS

CHAPTER 1

TOUCHING THE SKY

Have you ever stacked blocks to build a tall tower?

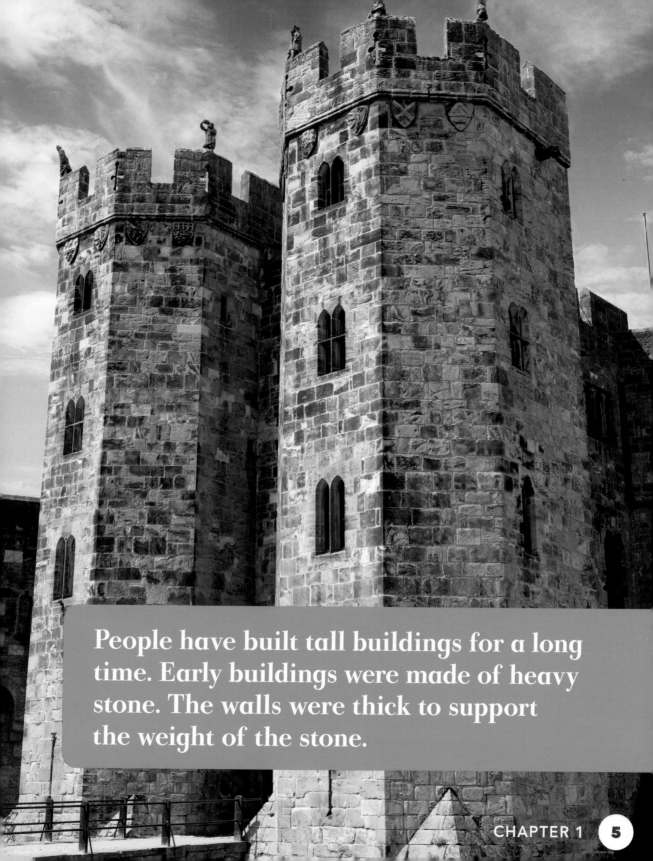

People have built tall buildings for a long time. Early buildings were made of heavy stone. The walls were thick to support the weight of the stone.

Today, most tall buildings are in cities. They are made of **steel**, glass, and **concrete**. They are called skyscrapers.

People work in skyscrapers. They live in them, too.

Space is limited in a city. Building up gives people more floor space. They can live and work in space that had once just been sky!

DID YOU KNOW?

To rise into the sky, a skyscraper must be rooted in the ground. That's why the first step in building up is to dig down. The basement is almost always the first part of a skyscraper to be built.

CHAPTER 2

THE FIRST SKYSCRAPERS

In the 1800s, important **inventions** made skyscrapers possible.

People found a way to make a lot of steel.

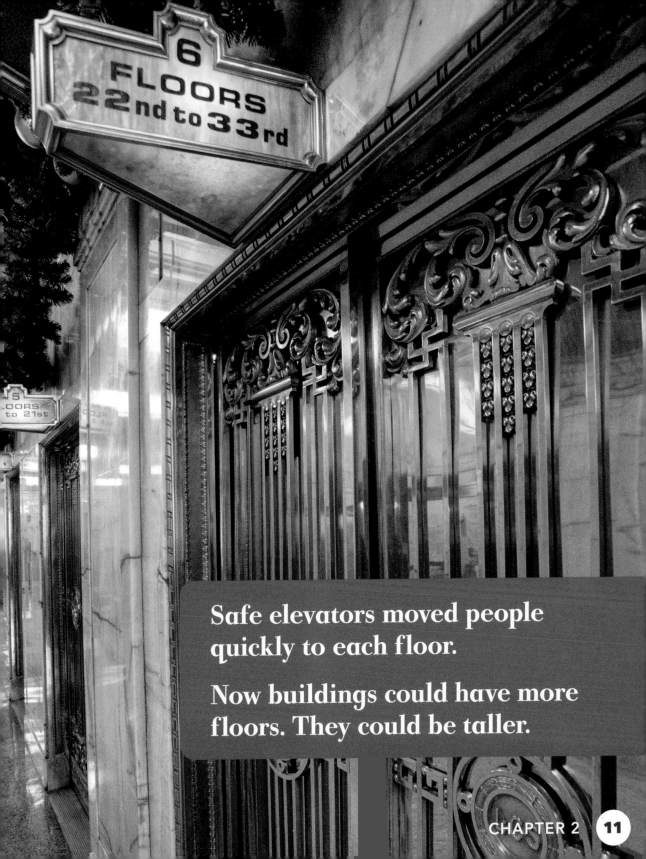

Safe elevators moved people quickly to each floor.

Now buildings could have more floors. They could be taller.

Burj Khalifa · · · · ▶

The first steel skyscrapers were in Chicago and New York City.

The Empire State Building in New York was the first building to have more than 100 floors.

The tallest skyscraper has 163 floors. It is called the Burj Khalifa and is in **Dubai**.

DID YOU KNOW?

The Burj Khalifa is half a mile (.8 kilometers) tall. How tall is that? That's as tall as 725 second graders standing on top of one another. That's tall!

CHAPTER 3

BUILDING SKYSCRAPERS

Skyscrapers are built around a steel **frame**. It is made of **beams** and **columns**.

The frame supports the weight of the building and everything inside it.

It resists the pull of **gravity**. It also must stand up to wind and earthquakes.

Who builds skyscrapers?

Architects draw the building. They decide how it will look. They decide how many floors it will have.

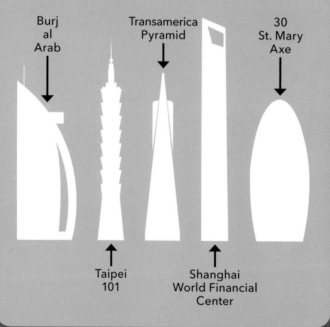

TAKE A LOOK!

Check out some skyscrapers known for their unusual shapes:

Burj al Arab

Transamerica Pyramid

30 St. Mary Axe

Taipei 101

Shanghai World Financial Center

architect

Engineers decide how strong the steel frame needs to be.

Building inspectors go inside. They make sure the building is safe.

DID YOU KNOW?

The Petronas Twin Towers is in **Malaysia**. A bridge connects the towers. It helps the towers stay more stable in strong winds. If there's a fire in one tower, people can cross to the other one.

engineer

building inspector

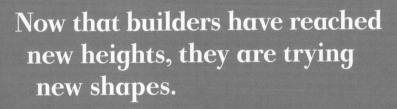

Now that builders have reached new heights, they are trying new shapes.

What do you think skyscrapers will look like in the future?

Do you want to build one?

Who knows? Maybe you will live in a skyscraper you built!

ACTIVITIES & TOOLS

TRY THIS!

BUILD A SKYSCRAPER

**Build a skyscraper with boxes you find around the house.
You will need:**

- boxes of different shapes and sizes, such as empty shoe or cereal boxes
- glue or tape
- acrylic paint and brushes
- newspaper
- measuring tape

1 Cover your workspace with paper. Paint your boxes. You don't have to paint the sides that you won't see. Set them aside to dry. These are your blocks.

2 Stack your blocks in different ways. Have some fun! Pretend to be an architect and draw your building first. When your skyscraper looks the way you want, glue the blocks together.

3 Your skyscraper is finished! Measure it. How tall is it? How many windows does it have? Take a picture of it. Great job!

GLOSSARY

architects: People who design skyscrapers and other structures.

beams: Long horizontal pieces of squared metal that span a building.

building inspectors: People who study buildings to make sure they are safe.

columns: Long vertical pillars of metal that support a building.

concrete: A mix of broken stone or gravel, sand, cement, and water, that hardens after it is spread or poured.

Dubai: The largest city in the United Arab Emirates, a country in the Middle East.

engineers: People who help plan and build skyscrapers and other structures.

frame: The metal structure that supports a skyscraper.

gravity: A force that pulls one object to another; for a building, it's the downward pull of the building toward the earth.

invention: A method, tool, or machine that is created for the first time.

Malaysia: A country in Southeast Asia that is made up of a peninsula and many islands.

steel: Metal made from iron and carbon.

INDEX

TO LEARN MORE

Learning more is as easy as 1, 2, 3.

1) Go to www.factsurfer.com

2) Enter "skyscrapers" into the search box.

3) Click the "Surf" to see a list of websites.

With factsurfer, finding more information is just a click away.